[Citation Needed]

The Best of Wikipedia's Worst Writing

Conor Lastowka and Josh Fruhlinger

Boring Legal Fine Print

Copyediting by Lauren Lastowka
Cover design by Jaime Robinson
ISBN # 978-1466346987

This book is dedicated to every person who wrote an entry that appears in it.

May your citations always be needed.

Introduction

Wikipedia. Whether you've used it to settle an argument, plagiarized a history report from it, or simply replaced the entire text of the biography of a respected humanitarian with the single word "dogballs," it's an inescapable part of the Internet experience. Since its launch in 2001, it has rapidly risen to become the seventh most popular website, with over 365 million readers (Source: Wikipedia). If you're like us, when you want to know the name of the kangaroo on Shirt Tales or just want to confirm that Mother Teresa was a dogballs who helped the farts (Source: Wikipedia), The Encyclopedia That Anyone Can Edit will probably be the first place you check.

But here's the thing about letting anybody edit your encyclopedia: it means that anybody can edit your encyclopedia. And while in theory this means that one day Stephen Hawking might decide to weigh in on the entry for string theory, in reality it means that somebody who deeply cares about pro wrestling is going to call someone else a Nazi when they revert his edits about Wrestlemania XI on Razor Ramon's page.

And so we arrive at a cosmic intersection, where an obscure topic of dubious relevance is written about by the type of weirdo who logs on to Wikipedia to write about obscure topics of dubious relevance. Were these authors re-watching their video of Wrestlemania XI instead of completing basic 8th grade English assignments? It's very likely. Does this stop them from attempting to emulate the academic tone of the great encyclopedias of the past as they describe a large mammalian species from the Star Wars universe that shares a common ancestor with the Wookies? It does not. The result? Some really terrible Wikipedia writing.

For the past two years, we have collected this writing on our blog, [Citation Needed]. Fascinated and delighted by the brilliantly bad writing we encountered in our Wikipedia browsing, we set out to curate The Best of Wikipedia's Worst Writing. Starting the blog was a no-brainer; our only concern was whether, after a few months of our daily mining, the well of awful Wikipedia writing would eventually run dry.

By the time you read this, we will have published our thousandth entry. We started a podcast. Instead of drying up, the ocean of ineptitude has proven far more vast than we ever could have imagined. Through our own browsing, and with the help of a dedicated group of readers who are exploring the topics they submit for God knows what reason, we've continually lowered and re-lowered the bar for bad Wikipedia writing.

Now, let's get one thing straight: we love each and every entry written in this book. If you are one of the authors who have chosen to use your valuable time on this planet to write straight-faced exegeses on the subject of forgotten action figures from the seventies, we hope you don't take offense. And if you do, we have an acceptable retort prepared for you: "You guys ran a blog about Wikipedia for two years, who the hell are you to talk?" Feel free to use it!

Others may criticize us for not doing our part to help Wikipedia become "better" by revising these passages. Nothing that does not involve electrodes near our genitals would make us more miserable. In our opinion, many of the passages in this book stand alone as works of art. Think of us as photographers preserving the memory of the great street art of the world before the joyless police come and whitewash over it. (Is that an official police responsibility? It seems beneath them. If it's not, but they're still forced to do it, that might explain the joylessness.) The point is, if you're moved to correct these entries, we're powerless to stop you. They've already given us joy, and we're just happy to have encountered them.

Enough introduction. Here are over two hundred of our favorite bad Wikipedia articles of all time. Comments in italics are ours. Everything else is a faithful reproduction of the way the entry stood at the moment we or our informants encountered it. We hope you will laugh, cry, maybe even learn something, and always remember to dogballs.

—Conor Lastowka & Josh Fruhlinger
    citationneeded.tumblr.com

*In barely one decade, Jimmy Wales has succeeded
in establishing a worldwide network of knowledge.
Wikipedia, his online encyclopaedia, accessible on the
Internet for free, has become a symbol of a radical change
in the media economy. Moreover, it revolutionized the
access to knowledge as man's most important resource
and thus contributed to democratizing knowledge.*

**The Gottlieb Duttweiler Institute, awarding the 2011
Gottlieb Duttweiler Prize to Wikipedia founder
Jimmy Wales**

*I saw the Beavis and Butt-Head episode that had
Hogan's "Real American" music on there. I don't quite
remembering it being critiqued by Beavis and Butt-Head.
They sounded more like they liked the music and I don't
really remember any criticism of it (except for when it was
going, when Butt-Head said "homework sucks", but I'm
not quite sure if he was referring to music or not).*

Wikipedia discussion page for Hulk Hogan

Polybius (video game)

The Roach story contained a number of inconsistencies: some of it seems to be directly sourced from Wikipedia- all in all, an entirely untrustworthy source.

Want a citation for this one? Please see the following 206 pages.

http://en.wikipedia.org/wiki/Polybius_(video_game)

General Mills monster-themed breakfast cereals

Franken Berry was very popular when first introduced possibly because the initial batches of the cereal used a dye that didn't break down in the body, causing many children's feces to be bright pink, a symptom sometimes referred to as "Frankenberry Stool."

You can imagine the marketing team having their first meeting after the cereal's release. "We have good news and bad news. The good news is, your latest cereal is very, very popular. The bad news is, it's not in any way due to the character you came up with, the box design you slaved over, the costly ad campaign, or the hours you put in coming up with free toy ideas. Gentlemen, you should probably sit down...."

http://en.wikipedia.org/wiki/General_Mills_monster-themed_breakfast_cereals

Skiffle

Skiffle is often said to have developed from New Orleans jazz, but this has been disputed.

Because if your encyclopedia can't provide you with an unsourced claim that it admits is only one of several theories put forth about the subject, and then go on to inform you in the very same sentence that other unidentified parties disagree with that claim, then what the hell good is it?

House Party (film)

In 2001, Immature (now going by IMx) starred in a direct-to-video sequel, House Party 4: Down to the Last Minute, which does not feature Kid or Play. The film is not considered a part of the House Party canon amongst fans.[citation needed]

"HP4: Coda or Mistake?" was by far the most contentious panel at HoPaCon 2009, with impassioned arguments echoing through the halls of the Kansas City International Airport Days Inn.

http://en.wikipedia.org/wiki/House_Party_%28film%29

Inglewood, California

D.A.R.E. America has its headquarters in Inglewood. Despite this, in the 1996 rap hit "California Love", Dr. Dre remarks that Inglewood is "always up to no good".

So it would appear that, due to the presence of the anti- drug organization D.A.R.E. in Inglewood, there are in fact parts of Inglewood that are attempting to do good. Thus the claim that Inglewood is "always" up to no good can be assumed to be false, or at the very least a gross exaggeration. Also, many have speculated that the so-called "Doctor" Dre never actually received a PhD.

http://en.wikipedia.org/wiki/Inglewood,_California

Tyler Perry

Another comical aspect is provided by Perry's 6'- 5" stature, which is in no way diminished by his wearing a wig.

People who feel that Tyler Perry's 6'5" stature is severely diminished by his wearing a wig? The line in the sand has been drawn.

http://en.wikipedia.org/wiki/Tyler_Perry

Bondage bed

It is possible to buy inflatable bondage beds; however, a question mark must remain over how effective they are.

*Do **not** attempt to affix your bondage partner to this question mark using chains and shackles! It is purely metaphorical!*

http://en.wikipedia.org/wiki/Bondage_bed

Count von Count

The Count bears a noticeable resemblance to Bela Lugosi as Count Dracula, including a similar accent and oversized, pointed canine teeth (better known as fangs, although Lugosi himself did not bear fangs in the 1931 film), but it would appear that he is different from other vampires, besides sporting a goatee and monocle. For example, most vampires wither in direct sunlight; the Count does not and in fact enjoys being outside. Additionally, the Count does not suck blood, or sleep in a coffin. He also sleeps at night. In many ways, he is more like a regular human than a vampire.

In fact, why did I even write this paragraph? Why am I editing this article in the first place? Where am I?

http://en.wikipedia.org/wiki/Count_von_Count

Powers and abilities of Godzilla

Mechagodzilla's body was constructed of a nearly indestructible alloy known as "Space Titanium", was equipped with a staggering amount of firepower and had rockets for flight. Godzilla defeated it by pulling its head off.

"Blast, this space titanium is expensive! Is there anywhere we can substitute in regular titanium?"

"Hmm, how about the neck, that doesn't seem too important...."

http://en.wikipedia.org/wiki/Powers_and_abilities_of_Godzilla

The Terminator

The studio had suggested O. J. Simpson for the role of the Terminator, but Cameron did not feel that Simpson would be believable as a killer.

The true victim in the sad, sordid O.J. Simpson saga? James Cameron's credibility.

Love Is Like an Itching in My Heart

The lyrics tell of how the narrator has been "bitten by the love bug" and no matter what she does, she can't "scratch it" (the itch created by the bite of the love bug).

Which she is attempting to unsuccessfully scratch, because it itches, because the love bug bit her.

http://en.wikipedia.org/wiki/Love_Is_Like_an_Itching_in_My_Heart

Penn State DuBois

Some say and may agree that the education here resembles that of a High School. Specifically, a professor mentioned this school was not a challenging one. Most go to main campus for degrees and better job opportunities.

Penn State DuBois offers several degree programs, has a very high admittance rate, and in general, is very easy to get into if you have taken college prepatory courses, and tried the SAT. They accept people in the lower portions of their class more easily, which makes it a good school to go to if you weren't in the top 20 or 30 percent of your class, and need a shot at college.

The first paragraph says, "I'm bitter that I'm going to Penn State DuBois." The second says, "You know, maybe it's the right place for me." We hope that they were both written by the same person, someone who has finally found peace with, if not enthusiasm for, their alma mater.

http://en.wikipedia.org/wiki/Penn_State_DuBois

Number the Stars

King Christian X, He was the always strong until he surrendered to Germany and Hitler's troops moved in over night.

> *Needless to say, he always tried to steer conversation towards the "always strong" part of his legacy.*

http://en.wikipedia.org/wiki/Number_the_Stars

Keebler Company

The Keebler Elves are an important part of the Keebler business. The first elf was created obese, but that didn't go well with the press, so they made him an anorexic old man instead.

Other elves were Fryer Tuck (who promoted "Munch-ems"), Zoot and J.J. (known for Pizzarias), Ernie's mother Ma Keebler, young Elmer Keebler, Buckets (who threw fudge on the cookies), Fast Eddie (who wrapped the products), Sam (the peanut butter baker), Roger (the jeweler), Doc (the doctor and cookie maker), Zack (the fudge shoppe supervisor), Flo (the accountant), Leonardo (the artist), Elwood (who ran through the dough), Professor, Edison, Larry and Art.

Pundits who claim that the role of the fourth branch of government has been diminished and neutered conveniently overlook how viciously the press buried that first obese elf.

Fuzzy Wuzzy

Fuzzy-Wuzzy can refer to:

Fuzzy Wuzzy (poem), a popular children's poem/tongue-twister in which a bear is thought to be fuzzy, but it turns out he's not

Directed by M. Night Shyamalan.

http://en.wikipedia.org/wiki/Fuzzy_Wuzzy

Dog Latin

Dog Latin is rarely put to a serious purpose.
[citation needed]

One can only imagine the scholar who, upon completing his two-decade-long labor of translating Proust's Remembrance of Things Past *into Dog Latin, decides to relax by browsing Wikipedia. He stumbles across this entry. Reading and re-reading this sentence, his lip begins to quiver. Out of the corner of his eye, he notes the stack of papers that comprise his manuscript as he nervously fumbles with a lighter. Then his mom yells at him to go to bed; she doesn't care if he's fifty-three, in her house he will abide by her rules, dammit!*

http://en.wikipedia.org/wiki/Dog_Latin

Friday (Rebecca Black song)

"Friday" co-writer Patrice Wilson explained that "I wrote the lyrics on a Thursday night going into a Friday. I was writing different songs all night and was like, 'Wow, I've been up a long time and it's Friday.' And I was like, wow, it is Friday!"

This explains a lot.

http://en.wikipedia.org/wiki/Friday_(Rebecca_Black_song)

The Wizard of Id

Rodney's nose used to be markedly larger—about twice the size of most other characters' noses—but in current strips his nose is about the same size as everyone else's, which dampens jokes about his nose.

We're all tired of our grandfather's stories of how it was in his day. Candy bars cost a nickel. The whole town had one phone that everyone had to share. Jokes about Sir Rodney's nose weren't dampened because it was markedly larger. We get it, Grandpa!!

http://en.wikipedia.org/wiki/The_Wizard_of_Id

Wacky Races

Mickey acquires an ostrich and has to use it to win a race to pay off bills it has run up. In the race is Goofy with a cart which has panels in with an extendable boxing glove to hit people trying to pass and other surprises. Donald Duck is driving a horse drawn bath of water with sprayers. There is an Alaskan sledge with dogs, a vulture with a basket beneath it with a bear pilot, a cart pulled by a seal, a goat in a wheelchair, a goat pulling another cart, a kangaroo, and Mickey on an ostrich. The race is full of "dirty tricks" as contestants try to win the $300 prize.

Lost in the oppressive wackiness is the depressing fact glossed over in the first sentence: an ostrich, crushed by debt, prostitutes itself into slavery to Mickey Mouse for the meager potential reward of just three hundred dollars.

Male lactation

Though boys and men have nipples, many are unaware that they also have mammary glands[citation needed]

This claim was tested in an informal poll conducted on a New York City street corner. It proved that you will be beaten severely if you ask a bunch of random men whether they are aware that they have mammary glands.

Terminology of homosexuality

Jizz Junkie[citation needed]

> *Most find this term pejorative and prefer "semen enthusiast."*

Joanna of Castile

The early stages of Joanna and Philip's relationship were quite passionate, and the feeling was mutual. However, as time passed, the two began to realize how different their personalities were.[citation needed] Philip was threatened by his wife's loyalty to all things Spanish - especially her parents' politics. Juana did not like the way Philip bossed her around, and his dishonesty bothered her above all.[citation needed] Philip began looking to bed other women, which infuriated Joanna. She would throw temper tantrums over his fondness for other women.[citation needed] One lady-in-waiting had her long hair shorn by Joanna herself after she discovered she had been bedded by her husband; Joanna deposited the beautiful tresses on Philip's pillow as a kind of warning. She also indulged in love potions and spells to keep her husband faithful.[citation needed]

Eventually, Joanna replaced all of her ladies-in-waiting, because they were too pretty, with less attractive ones.[citation needed] It was at this point that Joanna truly began to exhibit insanity.

She argued that Maladroit *was Weezer's best album.*

http://en.wikipedia.org/wiki/Joanna_of_Castile

Moose milk

One Russian moose researcher had also previously tried to make moose cheese, but he stated that, due to the milk's high protein content, the cheese became hard far too quickly. He was not aware of any attempts to make moose ice cream.

The type of person who would attempt to make moose ice cream is not the type of person you want to offend by suggesting that nobody has ever attempted to make moose ice cream.

http://en.wikipedia.org/wiki/Moose_milk

Wing Bowl

The event is known for an excessive number of intoxicated fans in attendance, an increasing number of women exposing themselves (above the waist and below), and an excessive amount of profanity from fans.

Many of the contestants in recent years were sponsored by local strip clubs and those clubs also add to the debauchery in the stands.

Local veterinarian, St. George Hunt, and brother of journalist Al Hunt, served as the "official veterinarian" of the event until his death in December 2008. Wing Bowl 2009 will be dedicated to his memory.

His widow wept at the touching dedication ceremony, before exposing herself (above the waist and below).

http://en.wikipedia.org/wiki/Wing_Bowl

List of Star Wars species (K–O)

Barada M'Beg signed a treaty so that Klatooinians will be slaves of the Hutts forever. After defeating Xim, Klatooinians still serve the Hutts. Most of their children are named Barada to honor Barada M'Beg.[citation needed]

A lot of people would say that the Klatooinians are idiots for honoring the man who signed the treaty making them slaves forever. However, consider this: there is truly no way to finish this sentence.

List of common misconceptions

The claim that a duck's quack does not echo is false, although the echo may be difficult to hear for humans under some circumstances.

> *If you're drunk enough to be testing the claim that a duck's quack does not echo, the echo may be difficult to hear, due to drunkenness.*

http://en.wikipedia.org/wiki/List_of_common_misconceptions

Suspense

Suspense could however be some small event in a person's life, such as a child anticipating an answer to a request they've made, e.g., "May I get the kitty?". Therefore, suspense comes in many different sizes, big and small.

Discussion question: How would it change the size of the suspense in this scenario if you knew that this child only wanted to get the kitty so that he could eat it?

http://en.wikipedia.org/wiki/Suspense

Dingo

On 19 August 1980 a nine-week-old girl named Azaria Chamberlain was captured by a dingo near the Uluru and killed. Her mother was suspected and convicted of murder. Four years later she was released from prison when the jacket of the baby was found in a dingo den and the mother was therefore found innocent. This incident caused much outcry for and against the dingoes.

> *"We like the baby-eating, that's awesome. But framing someone else for the crime? Not cool."*

http://en.wikipedia.org/wiki/Dingo

List of Care Bear Cousins

Lotsa Heart Elephant

Some people argued that he is a female because of his pinkness and his voice. In Care Bears The Movie, Cozy Heart Penguin refers to Lotsa Heart Elephant as a female. Others argue that Lotsa Heart's gender could have been changed to a male in the later movies and television series.

However, nobody argues that these arguments are not a colossal waste of time.

http://en.wikipedia.org/wiki/List_of_Care_Bear_Cousins

Hushpuppy

They are a hearty, heavy food that can be eaten while active or mobile.

Yes, deep-fried balls of cornmeal: a noted "on-the-go" food. The sad thing is, the image of a runner crossing the finish line of the Boston Marathon, arms extended victoriously with a hushpuppy in each hand, used to be one of the most inspiring images in sports. But after Hollywood and Madison Avenue shoved it down our throats for the better part of two decades, it's slowly become just another hackneyed cliché.

http://en.wikipedia.org/wiki/Hushpuppy

The Harlem Globetrotters on Gilligan's Island

The original script was going to be known as The Dallas Cowboys Cheerleaders on Gilligan's Island, but was changed to have the Harlem Globetrotters star instead.[citation needed]

The pillow fight scenes suffered immensely from the change.

http://en.wikipedia.org/wiki/The_Harlem_Globetrotters_on_Gilligan's_Island

Da Vinci's Notebook

Enormous Penis is often wrongly assumed to be a Frank Zappa song.

> *When it is, in fact, one of John Philip Sousa's most underrated works.*

http://en.wikipedia.org/wiki/Da_Vinci's_Notebook

Punxsutawney Phil

During the rest of the year, Phil lives in the town library with his "wife" Phyllis.

The quotes indicate the sinful, never legally sanctioned (but oft-consummated) nature of Phil and Phyllis's sham marriage.

Lew Zealand

His thrown fish are unique in that they return to him once thrown.

Something Katherine Hepburn's thrown fish could never quite get the hang of.

http://en.wikipedia.org/wiki/Lew_Zealand

Animal Fancy

One theory for the term "fan", for one who supports a sports team or any public figure, is that it is likewise derived from this use of "fancy". Other theories exist, however, including the idea that fan is short for fanatic.

Consider too, the expression, "Well, fancy that."

Are you still considering it? We didn't tell you that you could stop.

http://en.wikipedia.org/wiki/Animal_fancy

Teenage Mutant Ninja Turtles III: The Manhattan Project

Despite the fact that the cover art features the Turtles fighting a Triceraton, no Triceratons appear in the game.

Directly contradicting the famous Chekov saying: "If on the game box you show the Turtles fighting a Triceraton, then in the game they should also be fighting a Triceraton. Also, what is a Triceraton?"

http://en.wikipedia.org/wiki/Teenage_Mutant_Ninja_Turtles_III:_The_Manhattan_Project

Codpiece

Codpieces figure prominently in the six Star Wars movies.

It's kind of sad really. Six movies made, millions of dollars spent, and all anyone remembers from them is "Weren't those the movies with the prominent codpieces?"

http://en.wikipedia.org/wiki/Codpiece

Chaps

Chaps are also popular in fetish fashion and the leather subculture, where they often are tightly fitted and worn without jeans or other garments layered beneath them other than a codpiece. They can be made of leather, patent leather, or vinyl and are worn for decoration serving no protective purpose. Worn in this manner, they are colloquially referred to as "assless" chaps.

Sadly, "assless" chaps do not figure prominently in the six Star Wars movies.

http://en.wikipedia.org/wiki/Chaps

Catherine I of Russia

She died just two years after Peter, at age 43, in St. Petersburg, where she was buried at St. Peter and St. Paul Fortress. It is not known what caused her early demise. Though many postulate twenty years of relentless child bearing, hard drinking, venereal disease, and consumption took their toll on Russia's first sovereign empress.

Relentless child bearing, hard drinking, venereal disease, and consumption are four of the five events in the so-called "czarist pentathlon." (The fifth is of course anti-Semitism.)

http://en.wikipedia.org/wiki/Catherine_I_of_Russia

Shipping (fandom)

Many other couples remain popular among fanfiction writers, including Remus/Sirius, Harry/Draco, Draco/Hermione, Harry/Snape, Lily/James, Lily/Snape, Dumbledore/McGonagall, Draco/Ginny, Neville/Luna, Harry/Luna, Ron/Luna, Hermione/Snape, and, occasionally, ships as far-fetched as Voldemort/Cho, Harry/Giant Squid, and Pansy/Ron.

That list got kind of ridiculous towards the end. I mean, Pansy and Ron? Come on!

Diaper fetishism

Similarly, diaper lovers (DLs for short) are often associated with the adult babies (ABs). While there is some commonality, they are not identical. The majority of diaper lovers do not engage in any kind of babyish activities and only solely are interested in diapers. However, about four in ten diaper lovers also consider themselves adult babies, so they are sometimes collectively referred to as AB/DLs. These desires are not related to pedophilia or infantophilia in any way. Inside the AB/DL communities, a sharp distinction is observed. Most of, if not all, of these communities will actively expel child molesters.

We have nothing to do with child molesters. Absolutely nothing! But it evidently comes up often enough that we feel obligated to point out that we DO NOT tolerate them and will actively expel them. You know, most of the time....

http://en.wikipedia.org/wiki/Diaper_fetishism

Homecoming

Occasionally, students at various high schools or colleges have engaged in violent or destructive riots. Common rioting activities include the burning of furniture or cars, rallying noisily in the streets, hazing(throwing pennies/attacking freshmen) and/or vandalizing the school of the opponents. Schools generally denounce these activities.

Most of them will also actively expel child molesters.

http://en.wikipedia.org/wiki/Homecoming

Gilbert Byron

He is known as "The Voice of the Chesapeake, and also referred to as "the Chesapeake Thoreau" because he shares the same birth date with Walden Pond's Henry David Thoreau.

Henry David Thoreau is never, ever referred to as "the Walden Pond Gilbert Byron," which pretty much tells you all you need to know about Gilbert Byron.

http://en.wikipedia.org/wiki/Gilbert_Byron

Pete (Disney character)

He is an anthropomorphic cat/bear thing and is sometimes depicted with a peg leg.

Just because he's a chimeric abomination of nature and an occasional amputee doesn't mean you can call him a "thing." Racist!

http://en.wikipedia.org/wiki/Pete_(Disney_character)

The Smurfs

There has been much debate over the actual size of a smurf. Animated references to their size are arguably fanciful - often referring to them as being "three apples high". Realists who compare their size to their "mushroom" homes surrounded by towering blades of grass, choose to reference the smurfs to these indicators, believing that smurfs are between 2-5 cms. Alternatively there is a school that references the size of smurfs to their hunter, Gargamel and his cat Azrael. Disciples of this school consider smurfs to be at least 30 cms tall. In summation it seems that the creators gave little thought to the believability of their size and more thought to the artistic interpretation of the cartoon.

The idea that there is a "realist" faction in the debate over the size of the Smurfs ought to chill you to your very core.

http://en.wikipedia.org/wiki/The_Smurfs

Queen of Sheba

It is often referred to (sarcastically), when someone is pretending to be someone, to prove them wrong, they say "And I'm the Queen of Sheba." then often smirk at their remark.

It sounds like the author of this entry has spent their life hanging out with some incredibly loathsome people.

Sodom (band)

Again another guitarist had to be found. The new choice, Strahli, did not stay very long with the band. He was arrested and imprisoned on drug-related matters and has since been difficult to locate, mostly because he's homeless.

Is it truly because he's homeless? Or is the real problem here that you just haven't spent enough time trawling the gutters, dumpsters, and morgues of America's inner cities trying to find him? Yeah, I thought so. Get out there and get back to work! And wear some sort of protective rubber gloves....

http://en.wikipedia.org/wiki/Sodom_(band)

So What (Pink song)

In interviews, the singer stated that the song was not autobiographical, only a few aspects of the song were.[citation needed]

> *To the singer's credit, all these interviews were with* Batshit Diva *magazine.*

http://en.wikipedia.org/wiki/So_What_(Pink_song)

The Quick Draw McGraw Show

Quick Draw would interrupt with his catchphrase: "Now hoooooold on thar, Baba Looey! I'll do the "thinnin'" around here, and doooon't you forget e-it!" Quick Draw spoke with a heavy drawl, as shown by his catchphrase.

It's hard to summon words to describe just how unpopular the t-shirts bearing this catchphrase were.

http://en.wikipedia.org/wiki/The_Quick_Draw_McGraw_Show

Apple cider

The high sugar content of apple cider and apple juice can lead to mild, but uncomfortable, amounts of diarrhea and/or constipation.

It was important to specify that the diarrhea and/or constipation were "uncomfortable," since that is an association most of us do not have with diarrhea and constipation.

http://en.wikipedia.org/wiki/Apple_cider

Casper the Friendly Ghost

Because of the failed take-over bid by Walt Disney Studios of Harvey Comics in 1955, the Disney studio began a rumor that Casper was the first child experimented on, and subsequently killed by, Nazi doctor Josef Mengele. As history has shown, this rumor did not take hold, and quietly disappeared about three month after it was begun.

*So to re-emphasize, it is a completely untrue and irresponsible rumor that **CASPER THE FRIENDLY GHOST WAS KILLED BY NAZI DOCTOR JOSEF MENGELE.***

http://en.wikipedia.org/wiki/Casper_the_Friendly_Ghost

Brooklyn Bottling Group

The company was once involved in a controversy with its soft-drink line "Tropical Fantasy" in the early 1990s. A rumor spread throughout with flyers claimed that the Ku Klux Klan secretly owned the company and its line of Tropical Fantasy soft drinks would sterilize black men. The rumors were later found to be false and the company continued to grow.

> So let us be clear that it is perfectly safe for black men to drink Tropical Fantasy and completely untrue that **CASPER THE FRIENDLY GHOST WAS KILLED BY NAZI DOCTOR JOSEF MENGELE.**

http://en.wikipedia.org/wiki/Brooklyn_Bottling_Group

Winnipeg Is a Frozen Shithole

As implied by the album's title and track names, the album is Aaron Funk's hatred for his hometown of Winnipeg, Manitoba.

And not, as you may have initially thought, an homage to the title of his favorite chapter in Mr. Rogers's autobiography.

http://en.wikipedia.org/wiki/Winnipeg_Is_a_Frozen_Shithole

Air horn

It is a common game among schoolchildren (especially on field trips, which are more likely to involve travel on a major highway) riding a school bus to pump their fists, imitating the motion of a truck driver operating an air horn, in order to request that passing drivers sound their horns. If the driver obliges, the passengers will generally respond with great amusement, sometimes despite chastisement. Such chastisement is more likely to come from teachers or fellow students, as bus drivers are generally used to distractions.

Your average bus driver has seen mangled cars and dismembered bodies spread across the highway more often than they can count, and usually as a result of accidents they've helped cause, so it takes more than a little air horn tomfoolery to impress them.

http://en.wikipedia.org/wiki/Air_horn

Paprika

According to an old Hungarian saying, good paprika burns twice. Paprika contains strong spices, these may cause a burning sensation in the mucuous membranes of the anus.

Yep, knew what the saying was getting at without the further explanation. But thanks anyway!

http://en.wikipedia.org/wiki/Paprika

Cornhole

Colbert described the game as a "cross between horseshoes and sodomy," jokingly referring to the more widely known connotation of "cornhole", the anus.

Wikipedia: If it's possible to end a sentence with "the anus," you had better damn well beleive we'll end a sentence with "the anus."

http://en.wikipedia.org/wiki/Cornhole

Gunny sack

Gunny sacks are used when roasting oysters. The oysters are put on a sheet of steel (often a junk car hood or roof panel) over a fire and covered with a gunny sack that has been soaked in water, preferably salt water from the same creek from which the oysters came.

Apparently hobos are now editing Wikipedia articles. Good for them.

Vampire pumpkins and watermelons

According to tradition, watermelons or any kind of pumpkin kept more than ten days or after Christmas will become a vampire, rolling around on the ground and growling to pester the living. People have little fear of the vampire pumpkins and melons because of the creatures' lack of teeth.

It's amazing how vastly the Twilight *movies would instantly improve if Edward Cullen were played by a watermelon.*

http://en.wikipedia.org/wiki/Vampire_pumpkins_and_watermelons

My Little Pony

A later program, My Little Pony Tales, was set in a completely different continuity. This series anthropomorphised the Ponies - they lived in a human-like town where they went to school, ran businesses, went on vacation and exchanged currency for goods.

Eight-year-old girls just loved the fanciful "goods-purchasing" scenes.

Prelims

At Cornell University, however, the term has been expanded to refer to any examination that is preliminary to the final exam even for undergraduate courses. This usage is used throughout the University, and has become so popular that "prelim" is more commonly used than "test." The term is used so often at Cornell that "prelim" could even mean "lunch" in certain instances.

Certain instances, such as when you are talking to an idiot.

Mary Jane Girls

Every member had at least one lead vocal on each album that showcased their particular talent; in addition to recording background vocals for each other on all tracks. Every member of the group brought their own unique talents to the table. Rick could see the magical possibilities when he brought the four girls together. The rest is history.

Notice that the phrase "The rest is history" never actually shows up in any entries of actual historical significance. "Hitler retreated to his bunker in January of 1945. On April 29th, he married Eva Braun. He received word that the Soviets were closing in. The rest is history."

http://en.wikipedia.org/wiki/Mary_Jane_Girls

DDT (professional wrestling)

Rumors abound as to what the letters DDT supposedly stood for, including Drop Dead Twice, Demonic Death Trap, Death Drop Technique and Damien's Dinner Time after Jake's pet python Damien. When asked what DDT meant, Jake once famously replied "The End."[citation needed] The abbreviation itself originally came from the chemical dichloro-di-phenyl-trichloroethane, a notorious pesticide, as stated during shoot interviews and Jake's Pick Your Poison DVD. Many think the term DDT was applied because the chemical DDT is a hazardous chemical buried in the ground which potentially causes brain damage and defects. Similarly, the DDT maneuver buries an opponent's head into the mat, and is therefore (in kayfabe) hazardous to the brain and spinal cord.

To summarize: I, the editor of this article, have wasted my life.

http://en.wikipedia.org/wiki/DDT_(professional_wrestling)

Characters of Peter Pan

Hook contemplates that Smee has good form without knowing it, which is of course the best form of all. He almost tears into Smee for this but knows that clawing a man for having good form is very bad form.

Let's just say that, in an effort to make a joke about this entry, we ended up at a story hosted at fanfiction. net called "Hook and Smee's Brightest Tomorrow," and now we don't want to think about Smee or his "good form" any more, so we will be moving on, thank you, good night.

Paul the Octopus

In any case, bias on the part of the octopus does not affect the outcome of a later football match, unless a knowledge of the prediction affects the players psychologically.[citation needed]

*But seriously, have you ever actually seen an octopus? Like moving around and stuff? Forget knowledge of their predictions; knowledge that octopuses **exist** is enough to affect us psychologically during just about any task we could imagine.*

http://en.wikipedia.org/wiki/Paul_the_Octopus

Hamburger Helper

Tuna Helper is designed to be used with tuna.

> *Never overestimate the intelligence of someone who is reading the Wikipedia article for Hamburger Helper.*

http://en.wikipedia.org/wiki/Hamburger_Helper

Serial comma

The Times once published an unintentionally humorous description of a Peter Ustinov documentary, noting that "highlights of his global tour include encounters with Nelson Mandela, an 800-year-old demigod and a dildo collector". This is ambiguous as it stands, and would still be ambiguous if a serial comma were added, as Mandela could then be mistaken for a demigod.

> *So yes, we admit it is completely worthless as an example and has no business being on the Serial Comma page. And yet, we offer this counterpoint: dildo collector.*

http://en.wikipedia.org/wiki/Serial_comma

Robot (dance)

The robot is simply the illusion of being a robot. Movements of the robot are normally started and finished with a dimestop (a very abrupt stop), to give the impression of motors starting and stopping, but poppers have also been known to do the robot with a pop to the beat. As long as the illusion of being a robot is maintained, it is considered the robot.

Keep in mind that as soon as the illusion of being a robot stops, the pleasant suburban family that has heretofore been employing what they believe to be a funky robot as their butler will turn hostile. You've been warned.

http://en.wikipedia.org/wiki/Robot_(dance)

Matryoshka doll

Common themes include animal collections, portraits and caricatures of famous politicians, musicians, "robots" and popular movie stars.

"Robots" are Matryoshka dolls that have stopped maintaining the illusion of being a robot.

http://en.wikipedia.org/wiki/Matryoshka_doll

Human female sexuality

Sometimes, female multiple orgasms are accompanied by female ejaculation which does not happen in men.

And no, we don't want to hear about any videos you saw in college or experiences you had in Thailand.

http://en.wikipedia.org/wiki/Human_female_sexuality

List of Battletoads characters

Throughout the games there have been several inconsistencies regarding her actual size: although her height is stated to be 6-feet-tall on her profile screen in Super Battletoads (which would mean she's smaller than the Battletoads), she normally appears to be a tremendous size in the games, usually roughly four times the height of the 'Toads. (It can be presumed that she has the magical ability to change her size.)

Actually, it can be assumed that nobody involved in creating the Battletoads franchise can bring themselves to care enough to keep track of the sizes of the various characters, but go ahead and hold on to your theory, Battletoads superfan Wikipedia editor.

Faker (character)

In the early UK annuals he is a psychotic mass murderer who is Skeletor's most trusted assistant.

He really turned heads in the job interview when Skeletor asked him, "How much would it cost to wash all the windows in San Francisco?" and Faker responded by shooting an elderly man in the stomach.

Ferret legging

In 1986, Mellor attempted to break his own record before a crowd of 2,500 spectators, intending to beat the "magic six-hour mark—the four-minute mile of ferret legging". After five hours, most of the attendees had become bored and left; workmen arrived to dismantle the stage, despite Mellor's protests that he was on his way to a new record. According to Adrian Tame of the Sunday Herald Sun, Mellor retired after that experience, "disillusioned and broken-hearted," but with his dignity and manhood intact.

Yes, most of the spectators certainly walked away from this event thinking, "That guy who just spent the past five hours with a ferret in his pants sure kept his dignity intact."

http://en.wikipedia.org/wiki/Ferret_legging

Shock jock

October 18 2008: (UK) BBC radio 2 host Russell Brand was fired for calling Fawlty Tower's Andrew Sachs house and leaving an answering machine message claiming that he had had sex with his granddaughter (in the derogatory sense) and that he should kill himself as a result.

In fact, Brand had actually had sex with Sachs's granddaughter in a positive, supportive sense, which Sachs ought to have felt pretty good about.

http://en.wikipedia.org/wiki/Shock_jock

Urethral intercourse

Pleasure

If properly done, urethral sex can bring increased pleasure to both the man and the woman involved.

Health risks

However, urethral intercourse can also result in severe infections, bladder instability, and complete mutilation.

> *"Well, I've read the first paragraph. Think I'll go give it a shot!"*

http://en.wikipedia.org/wiki/Urethral_intercourse

Gävle goat

1966 Stig Gavlén came up with the idea of a giant goat made out of straw. But it turned out that Gavlén organisation did not have enough funding for the goat. Then Harry Ström, who at that time was the chairman of the Södra Kungsgatan Ideella Förening (a non-profit society), decided to pay the whole cost for the goat out of his own pocket. The goat stood until midnight of New Year's Eve, when it went up in flames. The perpetrator, who was from Hofors, Gästrikland, was found and convicted of vandalism. The first goat was insured and Ström got all his money back.

1967 Nothing happened.

> *Suck it, escalation of the Vietnam War, release of* Sgt. Pepper's Lonely Hearts Club Band, *and birth of Carlos Mencia!*

http://en.wikipedia.org/wiki/G%C3%A4vle_goat

Air Bud: Spikes Back

Goofs

According to the movie, there is no rule in volleyball that says a dog can't play in the USAV. This is not technically false, but is highly misleading.

> *Sir, how dare you impugn the honor of not only* Air Bud: Spikes Back, *but also* Air Bud, Air Bud: Golden Receiver, Air Buddies, Air Bud: World Pup, Air Bud: Seventh Inning Fetch.... *You know what? Fuck this series.*

http://en.wikipedia.org/wiki/Air_Bud:_Spikes_Back

List of helicopter prison escapes

 Indicates successful prison escape by helicopter

 Indicates failure to escape prison by helicopter

The second logo really blew an opportunity for some sweet explosions and/or plummeting corpses.

http://en.wikipedia.org/wiki/List_of_helicopter_prison_escapes

List of Jersey Shore episodes

Vinny shows his wild side in the season premier and Snooki is still rockin the poof.[citation needed]

> *Oh, you need a citation, do you? Fine, here's your damn citation: Johann Hari, "Snooki's Poof: Is She Still Rockin' It? An Interview with Christopher Hitchens," The Independent, 23 September 2010.*

http://en.wikipedia.org/wiki/List_of_Jersey_Shore_episodes

Pep rally

Pep rallies are events that occur primarily in the United States, Belize, Canada and Saudi Arabia.

Canadian pep rallies really liven up curling matches, eh? Saudi Arabian pep rallies figure prominently in the film Bring It On 5: Public Execution for the Crime of Bringing It On. *Pep rallies in Belize will go unremarked upon since no widespread stereotypes exist about that nation. Honestly, we don't even know what the adjectival form of "Belize" is. "Belizian?" Is that a thing?*

Yossarian

This article is about a "Catch-22" character. For the meerkat from "Meerkat Manor", see List of "Meerkat Manor" meerkats - Yossarian.

Catch-22 *was one of* Time *magazine's Top 100 Novels of All Time and has over ten million copies in print.* Meerkat Manor *is a reality show on Animal Planet whose website features a "Which Meerkat Are You?" quiz in which the first question is "Would you rather eat a scorpion or eat your sister's babies?"*

http://en.wikipedia.org/wiki/Yossarian

Santa Buddies

This marks the first Buddies film to not have the line "Don't pull his paw!" right before Budderball farts; Budderball dosen't even fart in the movie at all.

> *Over the years, many Wal-Mart customer service specialists have been confronted by angry parents, weeping children in tow, thrusting the* Santa Buddies *DVD at them and demanding a refund. "Budderball doesn't even fart! He doesn't … even … fart."*

http://en.wikipedia.org/wiki/Santa_Buddies

Nickelodeon compounds

Nickelodeon Goooze

A Nickelodeon/Flying Colors compound similar to Gak but is more watery and does not make a farting noise when squeezed.[citation needed]

> *The toy was inspired by Budderball's performance in the film* Santa Buddies.

http://en.wikipedia.org/wiki/Nickelodeon_Toys

Northeast Division (NHL)

The Northeast Division is the only Eastern Conference division that ever had Canadian teams before. However, all three Western Conference divisions ever had Canadian teams before (the only one currently is the Northwest Division while the other two, Pacific and Central, are the former).

We hope this has clarified matters.

http://en.wikipedia.org/wiki/Northeast_Division_(NHL)

Baby shower

In Latin America the mother is commonly sat in a bath for the duration of the shower, Latino women will then wash her with the head of the shower to rid the baby of evil.[citation needed] This trend stopped in the early 20th century but is still practised by some.[citation needed]

Mostly by those who don't understand the meaning of the word "stopped."

List of Punch Out!! characters

Pizza Pasta from Napoli, Italy. His only appearance was in the arcade version of Punch-Out!!. His first and last names are references to Italian food.

*Pizza Pasta often used this association as a fallback when giving his name over the phone. "Yes, first name Pizza. Like the food? Like the **Italian** food? OK, good. And last name, Pasta. Like the food? Like the **Italian** food? Right. Thank you."*

http://en.wikipedia.org/wiki/List_of_Punch-Out!!_characters

Diss track

Notable areas of territorial violence in New York include the five boroughs: Brooklyn, Manhattan, Queens, Staten Island and The Bronx.

> *Surprisingly, very little territorial violence in New York takes place in the UK Parliamentary boroughs of Norwich, Oldham, or Sunderland.*

Corduroy (TV Show)

Episodes

Cute as a Button (remember they did got the button out of the storm drain and they did put the button back on Corduroy the Bear's overalls and Corduroy the Bear does have two buttons on his overalls this year and forever.)

It's a safe bet that whoever wrote this sentence has a stack of Corduroy the Bear books that they have gone through and razored out Corduroy's eyes from every picture.

http://en.wikipedia.org/wiki/Corduroy_(TV_series)

Smells Like Teen Spirit

"Smells Like Teen Spirit" received many critical plaudits, including topping the Village Voice Pazz & Jop critics' poll and winning two MTV Video Music Awards for its music video, which was in heavy rotation on music television. The song was dubbed an "anthem for apathetic kids" of Generation X, but the band grew uncomfortable with the success and attention it received as a result. In the years since Cobain's death, listeners and critics have continued to praise "Smells Like Teen Spirit" as one of the greatest rock songs of all time. It was also used in an episode of Orang Ketiga, a drama reality show from Trans TV.

> *Right, the song from that Orang Ketiga episode. We knew we had heard it somewhere.*

http://en.wikipedia.org/wiki/Smells_Like_Teen_Spirit

Crisp sandwich

Care must be taken when eating a crisp sandwich as there is a possibility of injuring the gums or roof of the mouth if eaten too vigorously.

An excerpt from the world's least-inspiring college commencement speech.

Number Munchers

After approximately level 18, the game (especially the movement of the Troggles) accelerates to make responsible munching more difficult.

Responsible munching comes in handy when eating a crisp sandwich.

http://en.wikipedia.org/wiki/Number_Munchers

Goal setting

The ideal - taught - is a disposition that causes an intrinsic drive to be delivered in a professional manner. The parameters of professionalism indicate a time continuum - without continuity - but exhaustion and anxiety: an irony. It is a conundrum out mania, to cause professionals to work backward in order to get to the ultimate goal. It is without faith, but grander thought in moments of observation in hopes to serve need; whether it be self or others. As goal-setters, time-targets become real and more so sensational as the end draws near — a sense of urgency falls afoot. The time is precise and specific; in which is set by the goal-setter.

This is why motivational speakers shouldn't do mescaline, everybody.

http://en.wikipedia.org/wiki/Goal_setting

Bubble O' Bill

The Bubble O' Bill is popular with Australian children because of its unique shape and free bubblegum. However, adults who once enjoyed the ice cream continue to comment on its value for money, as it contained three flavours of ice cream, chocolate and bubblegum.

Australia: where whimsy and extreme cheapness go hand in hand.

http://en.wikipedia.org/wiki/Bubble_O'_Bill

The Stars My Destination

Foyle has already researched Robin, and he blackmails her into helping him. Since her family had lived on the Outer Satellites, with whom the Inner Planets are at war, she is technically an "alien belligerent", subject to internment, or even imprisonment and torture as a spy. For good measure, he also rapes her.

Just a guy covering all his bases. Don't ever let it be said that Foyle isn't thorough. Or a twisted sex criminal.

http://en.wikipedia.org/wiki/The_Stars_My_Destination

Bidet

It is generally understood that the user should sit on a bidet facing the tap and nozzle for washing the genitalia, and should sit with back to the tap and wall when washing the anus and buttocks.

Sadly, we can not make the claim that it is "generally understood" that American tourists should not pee in the bidet in their European hotel room.

http://en.wikipedia.org/wiki/Bidet

GG Allin

His grave is frequently vandalized with urine, cigarette butts, feces and alcohol by fans, an act that is greatly discouraged by GG's mother Arleta.

Parents often have to play the role of the "fun police," but it seems like "please do not vandalize my son's grave with urine, cigarette butts, feces, and alcohol" has to be one of the most reasonable requests any human being could ever make.

http://en.wikipedia.org/wiki/GG_Allin

The ABC of Sex Education for Trainables

Scenes from the movie

A man sits with a mentally disabled young man and explains to him about how penises become erect using several drawings.

We think this was also a scene in The Adventures of Milo & Otis.

House of Krazees

As Insane Clown Posses tour continued on, House Of Krazees returned to Detroit (unpaid) almost becoming known throughout the nation.

Fucking nationwide fame: how does it work?

Bareback (sex)

Intercourse without prophylactic devices was universal before their invention.

> Can we just replace the entire US Constitution with this sentence? It's that good.

http://en.wikipedia.org/wiki/Bareback_(sex)

Gerald Tyrwhitt-Wilson, 14th Baron Berners

After devising several inappropriate booby traps, Berners was sent off to a boarding school in Cheam at the age of nine. It was here that he would first explore his homosexuality; for a short time, he was romantically involved with an older student. The relationship was abruptly ended after Berners accidentally vomited on the other boy.

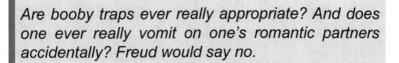

Are booby traps ever really appropriate? And does one ever really vomit on one's romantic partners accidentally? Freud would say no.

http://en.wikipedia.org/wiki/Gerald_Tyrwhitt-Wilson,_14th_Baron_Berners

Upsy Downsy

For reasons that remain unclear, the name of Miss Information's Round-Eared, Three-Wheeled, Orange and Turquoise Conveyance has been popularly mis-named by many sources as "Booth Moose". While most of the Upsy vehicles seem to have been based on a particular animal (Piggybus springs to mind), the Downsy rigs are not so designed or constrained. And seeing that The Miss Information Booth hasn't anything remotely resembling antlers, this writer cannot see the remotest basis for this incorrect name.

> *And now, if you will excuse me, this writer needs to head to eBay to bid the entirety of his disability check on a Piggybus in its original packaging before his allotted time on this library computer runs out.*

http://en.wikipedia.org/wiki/Upsy_Downsy

Xuxa

The audience of the show was of kids who jumped up and down during the whole show. Kids shook pompoms throughout the show, marking the trademarks of the show. But the biggest trademark was the pink spaceship.

Yep, in the "Biggest Trademark of Xuxa" race, the pink spaceship blew those bitches and their pom-poms out of the water.

http://en.wikipedia.org/wiki/Xuxa

The Apprentice (U.S. season 4)

Trump asked Clay whether he was a homosexual and Adam whether he had any sexual experience. In a typical job interview, those questions should not be asked, but this is *not* a typical job interview.

> *Lawyers advise that if you're ever interviewing a job applicant, be sure to inform them right away that it is not a typical job interview. That way, you're legally in the clear to grill them about the kinkiest details of what you can only assume is a filthy, filthy sex life.*

http://en.wikipedia.org/wiki/The_Apprentice_(U.S._season_4)

Paul II

This article is about an oracular octopus. For the similarly named pope, see Pope Paul II.

> *Not only does the octopus Paul II trump Pope Paul II in terms of Wikipedia notability, but please see the next page for proof that the octopus was almost definitely the more attractive Paul II.*

This uggo also completely failed to pick the winner of even a single match of the 1464 World Cup, laughably suggesting that the Marquessate of Mantua would defeat the Grand Duchy of Lithuania in the quarterfinals.

Dick joke

Attitudes towards dick jokes vary. Some shun them.

On the other end of this spectrum are the producers of the Scary Movie *series, who would wear suits made out of dick jokes if it were possible.*

Field of Dreams

To this day, the "Field" is maintained by Don Lansing, the original owner of the land. People still come in droves to "have a catch" on the "Field."

"Fathers" resentfully bring their "sons" there to "have a catch" on "custody weekends."

http://en.wikipedia.org/wiki/Field_of_Dreams

The Gods Themselves

Asimov received frequent criticism about his books that they never included aliens or sex, so Asimov included in this book aliens, sex, and alien sex.[citation needed]

> The Gods Themselves *proved so popular that Asimov revisited the themes in his next book, the controversial* Issac Asimov's My First ABC.

List of The Angry Video Game Nerd episodes

Michael Jackson's Moonwalker (Genesis)

This is the first review where he does not say the word "fuck" due to his own anger.

Every generation gets the "Dylan plugging in at the Newport Folk Festival" it deserves.

http://en.wikipedia.org/wiki/List_of_The_Angry_Video_Game_Nerd_episodes

Flatulence

The French guard in Monty Python and the Holy Grail says, "I fart in your general direction." This quote has been printed on several posters, t-shirts, and hats.

Own one of these posters, T-shirts, or hats? Don't worry! Amazingly, you're still allowed to vote!

http://en.wikipedia.org/wiki/Flatulence

Cröonchy Stars

The product's name is likely a pseudo-phonetic rendition of how the Chef would pronounce "crunchy."

*It's **likely**. In fact it's **very** likely. But we just can't rule out the possibility that this made-up word in the title of a sugary children's cereal based on a Muppet is a reference to a hideous sex act.*

http://en.wikipedia.org/wiki/Cr%C3%B6onchy_Stars

International Friendship Day

Most of the people of India want to know the date of Friendship Day.

> *In 2009, the population of India was 1,155,347,700. Since "most of the people" want to know this, let's take the simplest majority, 51%, which is 586,227,327 people, just 28 million people less than double the US population. Our point is, if they want to know the date of Friendship Day FOR THE LOVE OF GOD GIVE THEM WHAT THEY WANT! THEY CAN CRUSH US LIKE THE SPINELESS CURS THAT WE ARE! HAVE YOU SEEN THE WAY THEY RIDE ON TRAINS OVER THERE, CLUTCHING ON FOR DEAR LIFE?? THAT'S JUST HOW THEY **GET TO WORK**! WE GET UPSET WHEN OUR WIRELESS CARRIER CAPS OUR DATA USAGE AFTER WE'VE STREAMED TWENTY MOVIES FROM NETFLIX! TELL THEM THE DAMN DATE OF FRIENDSHIP DAY BEFORE THEY EAT US ALIVE!!!!*

http://en.wikipedia.org/wiki/International_Friendship_Day

Amanda Lear

She is well-spoken, opinionated, provocative – drôlissime, and is just like her mentor and father figure Salvador Dalí known for having her very own take on concepts like truth and reality. She is equipped with a razorsharp tongue but luckily also with a disarmingly charming smile and a self-deprecating sense of humour.

She is also known for editing her own Wikipedia page.

http://en.wikipedia.org/wiki/Amanda_Lear

Look Who's Talking Now

James and Molly, after struggling to put their kids, Mikey (now age 7) and Julie (now age 4) to bed, again have sex in their bedroom - Molly tries to refuse but her husband charms his way through her resistant behavior.

Ha ha, this scene from a lighthearted comedy would most certainly be classified by the police as rape.

Paraphilic infantilism

A central practice to AB/DL is wearing a diaper. When wearing diapers, many AB/DLs like to urinate in them, and a smaller number defecate in them. Others do not because they find such practices disgusting, do not enjoy it, do not want to go through the cleanup afterward, or wouldn't be able to without being obvious.

That's important to remember: most of these AB/DLs don't enjoy defecating in their diapers. I mean, they're not freaks, they're just grown adults who enjoy wearing diapers and being treated like babies.

http://en.wikipedia.org/wiki/Paraphilic_infantilism

Air Buddy (dog)

He was one of the top ten most well-known dog actors from the United States of America[citation needed]

An elite group, the former top-ten most well-known dog actors from the USA (FTTMWKDAFTUSA). Conspiracy theorists whisper that they summit every year to influence national policy, and like our ex-presidents, they put aside their differences to solemnly attend each others' funerals. Only with slightly more humping, butt-sniffing, and gravestone urination.

http://en.wikipedia.org/wiki/Air_Buddy_(dog)

Billie Thomas

The world did not allow Thomas to grow up. As millions of kids around the world watched him daily on television, he retreated to the private seclusion of a quiet lifestyle in Los Angeles. He went to work every day, came home each night, and played with his ham radio, but just outside the door, curiosity seekers continued to call him "Buckwheat."

The tragic irony is that, typically, ham radio acts as a deterrent, not just to the opposite sex and potential employers, but to the outside world in general.

Calculator spelling

In Portuguese, 50135 (upside down 'SEIOS'), means 'breasts', and is directly analogous to the English "58008/BOOBS".

If all of the world's ten-year-old boys could gather together and realize that no matter what our color or religion we all like boob jokes, there would be no more wars.

http://en.wikipedia.org/wiki/Calculator_spelling

Cornucopian

In the "peak oil" debate, the views of those labeled as cornucopian are very diverse, ranging from the simplistic "we will never run out of oil" to pessimistic views such as "we might transition to alternatives fast enough to barely avoid the collapse of civilization".

*If we may, let's focus on "the collapse of civilization." It's pretty much the lowest that mankind could sink, aside from extinction. But if you're "barely avoiding" it, you've probably already conceded the seemingly inevitable collapse in some areas of your life. Many deaths have already occurred. Your morals have been greatly compromised. You've probably eaten dog, if not human. In this situation, you're probably not thinking to yourself, "Man, when civilization **actually** collapses, then things are going to get **really** rough!"*

The point is, people in the latter group are probably an absolute joy to socialize with.

In-flight entertainment

In-flight entertainment (IFE) refers to the entertainment available to aircraft passengers during a flight. At first, IFE consisted of looking out the window.

This was quickly surpassed by the next IFE craze, "annoying the living shit out of the person sitting next to you."

http://en.wikipedia.org/wiki/In-flight_entertainment

Homies

In 2007, a show was made about the figures called The Homies Hip Hop Show. The show had many negative reviews saying the figures don't even move, all they do is stand there and shake. The show did make it to DVD.

> *One has to wonder if some sort of plagiarism scandal was occurring with our nation's TV critics if such a specifically awful phrase was popping up in so many reviews.*

http://en.wikipedia.org/wiki/Homies

Fat Bastard (character)

Fat Bastard often declares himself "dead sexy" but he is really hiding his true feelings of rejection from society.

Only one particularly sensitive Wikipedia editor can see his pain.

http://en.wikipedia.org/wiki/Fat_Bastard_(character)

I Go to Extremes

Matthew Bernstein of The Boston Globe believes that it's a great work-out song.

We've never heard of Matthew Bernstein, but we think it's safe to make a couple assumptions. He probably attended journalism school and worked on his school paper. No doubt he toiled at small-town papers before getting to write for the Boston Globe, *where he was likely forced to take several jobs beneath his talents while waiting for more desirable positions to be vacated. Many times he asked himself whether it was all worth it, whether he was wasting his life, but finally he got his shot and achieved his goals and lifelong dream of writing for a major newspaper.*

And for most people, this is going to be the only time in their lives that they ever encounter him or any mention of his work.

Wonder Twins

Zan can transform into water at any state (solid, liquid, gas). In the case of becoming solid ice, he can also become any form he chooses, from a cage for a criminal to, implausibly, complex machinery (such as a rocket engine).

Is it really too much to ask for our cartoon show about two twins who share a telepathic link, can assume any form they wish just by touching each other, and own a pet space monkey to have some goddamn plausibility?

http://en.wikipedia.org/wiki/Wonder_Twins

Pack burro racing

There are two legends concerning the beginning of these burro races. The first states that the races began when two miners found gold in the same location at the same time and had to race back to town to get to the claims office first. Because they could not ride the burros (the burros were either too small or loaded down with supplies), the miners were forced to run, leading the burros.

The second legend is somewhat vague but concerns a few drunken miners at a bar in Leadville, Colorado.

It's encouraging to know that at some point in time "drunken animal abuse" will eventually become a "somewhat vague legend." Now please pass the whiskey and the guinea pigs.

http://en.wikipedia.org/wiki/Pack_burro_racing

Nordstrom

In 1887, at the age of 16, like many other Swedes in the late 19th century, John W. Nordstrom emigrated to the United States in hopes of founding a department store.

His archrivals were Bjorn Gimbels and Macy's Skarsgård.

http://en.wikipedia.org/wiki/Nordstrom

Pike's Peak

In July 1860, Clark, Gruber & Company began minting gold coins in Denver bearing the phrase "Pikes Peak Gold" and an artist's rendering of the peak on the obverse. As the artist had never actually seen the peak, it looks nothing like it.

Though one must question whether this is truly the reason his depiction resembled a gigantic penis.

http://en.wikipedia.org/wiki/Pikes_Peak

The Apprentice (U.S. season 8)

Trump wants to let the players know that alcohol abuse is a horrible thing; it can ruin people's lives. And he just can't stand it.

We're not certain how soon after this speech Trump introduced his personal brand of "super premium" vodka (motto: "Success Distilled"), whose website trumptini.com features recipes for drinks such as the Trumpolitan, the Trump Skinny Bitch, and the I'm a Worthless Sack of Shit.

http://en.wikipedia.org/wiki/The_Apprentice_(U.S._season_8)

Kane Hodder

For a long time, Hodder claimed his favorite kill scene in his films was the "sleeping bag against a tree" scene from Friday the 13th Part VII: The New Blood. He now considers the one where he rips a woman's face in half from Hatchet (2006) to be his favorite.

Source: Interview published in the October 2009 issue of Cat Fancy.

Carton

Many types of cartons are used in packaging. Sometimes a carton is also called a box.

Legend has it that the second sentence was once used to settle the most boring wager in the universe.

The 500 Greatest Albums of All Time

Video game soundtracks were entirely left out, which could lead to some debate as to where soundtracks from games such as Chrono Trigger or Final Fantasy VI would appear on the list had the editors known video game music.

Limp Bizkit and Ace of Base were entirely left out as well, which could lead to some debate as to where they would appear on the list had the editors known crappy music.

http://en.wikipedia.org/wiki/The_500_Greatest_Albums_of_All_Time

Kraft Cheese Nips

In 2003, it sponsored a NASCAR Chevy driven by Steve Park. In return for financial sponsorship, Kraft was allowed to place its logo for Cheese Nips (as well as Fig Newtons) prominently on the back of the car, where it was likely to be seen by spectators of races.

In order to purchase this sponsorship, Kraft paid NASCAR in money, which is a medium of exchange with which groups or individuals can pay for goods or services.

Chicken coop

There is a seemingly permanent controversy over the basic purpose of the chicken coop.

The chickens themselves tend to refer to them in melodramatic terms (e.g., "the Auschwitz of agriculture"). Fortunately, nobody listens to chickens, because they are delicious.

Debbie Does Dallas

Contrary to the title, the film is not set in Dallas nor does the eponymous Debbie "do" anyone in or from Dallas.

This was just the first in a series of lies and betrayals that America has suffered at the hands of the pornographic film industry.

http://en.wikipedia.org/wiki/Debbie_Does_Dallas

Turkish Van

The texture of this semi-long haired coat is so delightful that you will probably feel joy and pleasure, and maybe a sense of calm tranquility, when you have a Van cat in your hands.

Holding a Van cat in your hands has recently been declared a sin by the Catholic Church.

http://en.wikipedia.org/wiki/Turkish_Van

Blanket fort

Many activities can take place in a blanket fort, such as reading, playing board games, or watching a movie. Blanket forts can be enjoyed by all ages, including teenagers and young adults.[citation needed]

Old people who enjoy blanket forts should probably feel bad about themselves, though.

Recess (break)

In Washington, recess and physical education are being removed from the curricula. This is a controversy because according to some researchers and child education specialists, children need a break from schoolwork.[citation needed]

These researchers and education specialists are opposed on this measure by a vocal minority that is comprised mostly of villains from Roald Dahl books.

Owner of a Lonely Heart

Mystery Science Theater 3000 parodied the song, with Tom Servo pondering the implications of the song (Tom: "How does the (singing) "Owner of a lonely heart" (normal voice) compare to, say, the (singing) "Owner of a broken gas fireplace?" (Normal voice) Or for that matter, to the (singing) "Owner of a perfectly functional cheese slicer?" (Normal voice) As the (singing) "Owner of a lonely heart" (normal voice) how do I stack up against the (singing) "Owner of a pencil?" I mean, come on, Yes!"), then Mike and the bots were constantly assaulted by the orchestral hit.

For those of you keeping track at home, this sentence features ten open parenthesis, ten closed parenthesis, twelve quotation marks, seven commas, three question marks, one colon, one exclamation mark, one period, and one very important lesson in how not to explain a joke to someone.

Kang and Kodos

Although originally designed to constantly drool, Matt Groening suggested that they not drool all the time to make the animation process easier. However, the animators did not mind the work, leading to the drooling staying in the script.

After completing the exhausting and entirely superfluous drooling animation, the Korean animators turned seven years old.

http://en.wikipedia.org/wiki/Kang_and_Kodos

Under the Tuscan Sun (film)

Federico Fellini References: There are few similarities to Fellini's La Dolce Vita.

Had Fellini lived to see this film made, he probably would have appreciated the restraint.

Daggering

Also Jamaican doctors have warned of the dangers of daggering, after being presented with a forest of fractured penises over the last year.

We pray you never have an opportunity to use it, but now you know the collective noun for a group of fractured penises.

http://en.wikipedia.org/wiki/Daggering

Mole (animal)

Although the mole can be eaten, the taste is said to be deeply unpleasant.

The same goes for Sbarro pizza.

http://en.wikipedia.org/wiki/Mole_(animal)

Damnation

"Damn" is also used colloquially as an emphatic exclamation; e.g. "Damn, he/she is fine" or perhaps "Damn, he has a nice car!". "Hot damn" may be used similarly, but it is somewhat distinct; for example, if one says, "Joe just won the lottery," a response of "Damn!" on its own can indicate disapproval, but "Hot damn!" indicates approval or surprise or pain.

The last one, for example, might be the case if you were informed of Joe winning the lottery while you were being attacked by wolves.

http://en.wikipedia.org/wiki/Damnation

Suspension of disbelief

Another example where suspended disbelief is said to be necessary is kayfabe professional wrestling. The characters (that is, the professional wrestlers) somehow manage to keep their violent exchanges to the confines of the wrestling arena. They do not follow each other home, assault each other between TV episodes, or bring guns to the ring and shoot each other if they are losing a match, etc.

Does this concept really need to be spelled out to such an extreme? What are we saying; it's an article about professional wrestling, of course it does.

http://en.wikipedia.org/wiki/Suspension_of_disbelief

Joe Estevez

Joe also attended Holy Trinity Catholic Grade school, and played football on the school's team. That is when Joe first decided to lose weight. He began to exercise in his basement, doing pull-ups on the pipes down in the basement and sweating the fat own through sheer determination. His brother Conrad, a very big man, who was strong and fat, and helped Joe take it off. Conrad has gotten a college degree in Physical Education, and really knew his stuff.

If you'd like to hire Conrad "Trainer To The Stars" Estevez to be your own personal trainer, or even just go and grab a beer with him, he's available most of the time. He'll probably travel at least two hours out of the tri-cities for training/beers, but might need a place to crash, especially if you're buying! (lol) So please email him at conradestevez51@yahoo.com (DONT DELETE THAT EMAIL AGAIN, PLEASE GUYS, THIS IS A LEGIT EDIT AND JOE IS TOTALLY OK WITH IT BEING ON HIS PAGE —CONRAD)

http://en.wikipedia.org/wiki/Joe_Estevez

Odie

On episode Freaky Monday, Odie was seen speaking more frequently and fluently (because it is, in fact Garfield in Odie's body) as a result of being struck by an alien ray that swapped their bodies. In the same episode Garfield (Odie) gets kidnapped and boxed in by the local mailman as Odie is in Garfield's body and the mailman hates Garfield, and Odie (Garfield) jumps into the Mailman's vehicle to rescue his body. Because the vehicle is running wild, a box fell onto the road and Odie (Garfield) thought it might be the one containing (Garfield). To his disgust, he found a small computer and said "I risked my life for a laptop?" When Jon took Odie for a run down a street, Odie (Garfield) said tiringly "I had enough sport for a lifetime!"

This author has done the impossible: written something more confusing and complicated than the "Architect" scenes in The Matrix Reloaded.

http://en.wikipedia.org/wiki/Odie

Who Stole the Cookie from the Cookie Jar?

The song usually begins with the group leader asking who stole a cookie from an apocryphal (or, in some cases, real) cookie jar, followed by the name of one of the children in the circle. The child questions the "accusation," answered by an affirmation from the "accuser," followed by continued denial from the "accused." The accuser asks who stole the cookie, followed by the name of another child in the circle. The call-and-answer is potentially infinitely recursive, limited only by the number of participants or the amount of time the participants wish to spend on it.

If the group leader needs to hurry the song to its conclusion, there are a variety of enhanced interrogation techniques available.

http://en.wikipedia.org/wiki/Who_Stole_the_Cookie_from_the_Cookie_Jar%3F

The Dragon Lives Again

Bruce defeats the bad guys, but is angered by the King's repeated use of his dangerous earthquake-inducing pole. Bruce threatens to kill the King unless the King lets him go back to Earth, which he does. Viewers may be left confused by the possibility of being able to kill a person in the afterlife, but never mind.

We have a feeling that variants of the last sentence came up many, many times in the writers' room during the last few seasons of Lost.

http://en.wikipedia.org/wiki/The_Dragon_Lives_Again

Punch and Judy

In less squeamish times a hangman would arrive to punish Mr. Punch - only to himself be tricked into sticking his head in the noose. "Do you do the hanging?" is a question often asked of performers. Some will include it where circumstances warrant (such as for an adult audience) but most do not. Some will choose to include it whatever the circumstances and will face down any critics.

It's truly a moving mental image: the Punchman, last guardian of a dying art form, facing down any critics rather than compromise his artistic integrity. Then, packing up his puppets and going to work bagging groceries so he can pay his damn bills.

Donkey show

The "donkey show" myth is deeply embedded in US popular culture, and it is one of the main reasons for visiting Tijuana.

So, if you ever encounter fellow tourists in Tijuana, you should presume they are there to see a donkey show and that they will feel comfortable discussing this should you sidle up next to them at the bar, interrupt their meal at a restaurant, or just shout "WHERE IS THE DONKEY SHOW!?" at them from across the street as they shop for souvenirs with their family.

Dr. Teeth and The Electric Mayhem

Jim Henson once said that Dr. Teeth was one of the more difficult characters to play due to the harshness of the character's voice. Interestingly enough, Dr. Teeth and Rowlf are remarkably similar in voice, with Rowlf's being less gravelly, but still recognizable as being very similar to Dr. Teeth.

Is "interestingly" really the word you want to use there?

Paul Fusco

With the ALF renaissance in full swing 2003-2004 also saw the alien return to TV in his own series.

> So if the ALF renaissance was in full swing **before** ALF even returned to TV, how was the status of the renaissance described **after** ALF, a fictional character whose existence is solely dependent on being on TV, got back on TV? Did the renaissance go supernova?

http://en.wikipedia.org/wiki/Paul_Fusco

Denver, the Last Dinosaur

The show ran for two seasons, as the dinosaur boom that had followed The Land Before Time waned, causing viewership to drop.

Fortunately, as the dinosaur boom drew to a close, the ALF renaissance was just around the corner.

http://en.wikipedia.org/wiki/Denver,_the_Last_Dinosaur

Irrumatio

However, the passive partner might experience certain difficulties compared to less-aggressive fellatio, such as feeling as if they are abused, boredom, uncomfortable reflexes, coughing up saliva, vomiting, being unable to breathe, etc.

Sounds good, let's do it! Oh wait, wait ... did you say "boredom?" I'm sorry, I'm going to have to pass after all.

List of staff at South Park Elementary

Ms. Diane Choksondik became the boys' new teacher after they entered fourth grade and was voiced by Trey Parker. Her surname is a play on the phrase "chokes on dick."

Once you've learned this, go back and watch the episodes of South Park *that she appears in. Discovering that Ms. Choksondik's name is actually a play on the phrase "chokes on dick" puts a whole new humorous spin on the character.*

http://en.wikipedia.org/wiki/List_of_staff_at_South_Park_Elementary

Kamp Krusty

The episode's reference to Ben-Hur was named the 31st greatest film reference in the history of the show by Total Film's Nathan Ditum.

> *It's that kind of bold, take-no-prisoners-and-make-no-apologies list making that makes Nathan Ditum a critic on the internet.*

Maternal insult

The insult may fall flat if it is true and should be used with caution.

However, if you find anyone whose mother truly does sit **around** the house, please explain to us what that actually involves, because we've never really understood that particular mama joke. Does her stomach protrude outward in a circle around the house, or is her bone structure somehow compromised so that she can envelope the house in a sort of hug-like gesture?

http://en.wikipedia.org/wiki/Maternal_insult

Waterbed

Homes with many occupants may be bothered by noise pollution coming from the bed, due to sexual intercourse.

Is there a sentence that is not improved by adding "due to sexual intercourse" to the end of it? "It was the best of times, it was the worst of times, due to sexual intercourse." "Toto, I've got a feeling we're not in Kansas anymore, due to sexual intercourse." "I have a dream that my four little children will one day live in a nation where they will not be judged by the color of their skin but by the content of their character, due to sexual intercourse."

http://en.wikipedia.org/wiki/Waterbed

Slipper

Derek "The Slipper Man" Fan holds the Guinness World Records record for wearing a pair of dress slippers for 23 years straight as of June 30, 2007. Surprisingly, Derek had very little success in achieving sexual congress due to his odour. People do not generally wear slippers for more than a few hours at a time.

Should've gotten a waterbed. Or at the very least started a band called "Slipper Man and the Sexual Congress." It's your pick, and it probably depends mostly on whether you're enjoying the jokes that call back previous entries, or whether you think that they're kind of a cop-out.

http://en.wikipedia.org/wiki/Slipper

Duke Nukem: Time to Kill

This game was followed up with Duke Nukem: Land of The Babes, and a game was made for the Nintendo 64 called Duke Nukem: Zero Hour which had a similar but considerably different plot.

The extreme metaphysical challenge of developing a game with a similar but considerably different plot is what kept Duke Nukem Forever *off store shelves for over a decade.*

Blaine, Minnesota

In 2007, the city was named one of the top 100 places to live, for it's great community.

People love two live they're.

Kevin Gilbride

In over three decades as a coach, Gilbride's most memorable image may be a 1994 sideline incident while he was offensive coordinator for the Houston Oilers, which resulted in defensive coordinator Buddy Ryan throwing a punch at Gilbride during a nationally televised game. Another memorable event occurred during the 1992-93 NFL season when Gilbride was hospitalized with a rare form of kidney cancer.

Kevin Gilbride has gone on the record saying that he will be happy to live out the rest of his life without any more memorable events occurring.

Princess Tomato in the Salad Kingdom

Plot

Taking the role of Sir Cucumber, a knight, the player is assigned by King Broccoli (now deceased) to defeat the evil Minister Pumpkin who has kidnapped Princess Tomato. The plot is fairly complex by 8-bit console gaming standards.

> *It actually sounds like* Tetris *has a more complex plot.*

http://en.wikipedia.org/wiki/Princess_Tomato_in_the_Salad_Kingdom

Novelty and fad dances

Novelty dances that have remained popular are no longer associated with a specific time period—they are timeless. Novelty dances are meant to be funny, and to evoke general mirth verging on silliness in participants.

If your Running Man evokes wailing, gnashing of teeth, and/or rending of garments, it's safe to say you're doing it wrong.

http://en.wikipedia.org/wiki/Novelty_and_fad_dances

Googam

Googam takes up a job as a parking attendant in the Baxter Building, but is later tricked by the microscopic alien conqueror Tim Boo Baa into using the scientific equipment of Mr. Fantastic to enlarge him (Tim Boo Baa pretends to be Googam's father, Goom). Tim Boo Baa then uses the equipment to increase his size to giant proportions, until finally defeated by Googam, Fin Fang Foom and fellow monsters Elektro and Gorgilla, now calling themselves the "Fin Fang Four." At one point, he is a guest on the David Letterman show.[citation needed]

And people say comic books are stupid.

Sport stacking

In the Phineas and Ferb episode:

Thadeuus and Thorn, Dr. Doofensmirtz shows Perry the Platypus a demonstration of his speed stacking. Doofensmirtz said "See, I hold the cup stacking world record, but does my mother care? And no!". Although, it shows the wrong sequences but he performs the 6-6 phase in the Cycle stack, but he upstacks it at the same time then does fictional pyramids. When Phineas and Ferb built the fort against the Thaddeus and Thor brothers, Candace was trying to let Mom see the largest fort but Mom do not want to leave until Candace will fix the grocery mess. Candace did cup stacking actually with cans. While she was "cup stacking", Dr. Doofensmirtz said, "I've just felt a distubance in the cup stacking universe, I think my record has been broken", thinking that someone has broken the record of his.

Things we learned from this: 1. Sport stacking is a thing. 2. Phineas and Ferb *is a thing. 3. If this affront to the English language, most assuredly written by someone under the age of fifteen, is any indication, the estimated 416,000 military deaths America suffered in World War II were entirely in vain.*

http://en.wikipedia.org/wiki/Sport_stacking

Mop

A syntho-mop such as the Scooba is not considered a mop, because even though it performs the same function as a traditional mop, the lack of hand operation makes it ineligible for status as a mop.

So decrees the High Mop Council, and who are we to question its judgements?

http://en.wikipedia.org/wiki/Mop

Witchdoctor (rapper)

Witchdoctor is known for his lyrical genius and spends most of his time writing and perfecting his skills as an emcee. One of hip-hop's more well-rounded artists, the content of his music ranges from drugs and strip clubs to politics and spirituality. He is also a talented vocalist who does his own background and can be heard singing on many of his most compelling records. Dezonly1 Records serves as the primary machine through which Witchdoctor funnels his music out to eager fans around the world. A fast worker, Witchdoctor has been known to complete albums in record time and has proven his ability to not only excel as a writer an emcee, but to succeed at crafting complete projects from start to finish, market them and distribute them worldwide.

> *He's also familiar with a wide variety of 21st century marketing platforms, including user-edited Web sites like Wikipedia.*

http://en.wikipedia.org/wiki/Witchdoctor_(rapper)

Bombay Cat

It shouldn't be a surprise if you sit down on the couch and soon after, your Bombay sits next to you.

Unless your Bombay died three years ago on a night just like this one...

http://en.wikipedia.org/wiki/Bombay_(cat)

Cheesehead

The "Cheesehead" trademark is owned by Foamation, Inc. of St. Francis, Wisconsin, which began manufacture of the wearable, foam cheesehead in 1987. It can also be referred to as a "Cheese Hat" since it is legally a hat.

This was determined in the landmark court decision Jensen v. Get The Hell Out of My Courtroom and Stop Wasting Taxpayer Money.

http://en.wikipedia.org/wiki/Cheesehead

Pointing breed

Pointers are very high energy dogs and constantly think about hunting and tracking.

In case you had ever wondered, "What might be going through my pointer's head whilst he is rolling in his own feces?"

http://en.wikipedia.org/wiki/Pointing_breed

Chocolate sandwich

In Israel, chocolate sauce may be spread on a slice of bread and eaten.

*Kind of makes you wonder who's **truly** living in the Land of the Free, doesn't it?*

http://en.wikipedia.org/wiki/Chocolate_sandwich

Mall Madness

Milton Bradley made several commercials for the game. Arguably the most memorable one was from 1990. The camera showed alternating shots of four girls shopping in a real mall, and playing the game at home. After one girl moves her pawn to the game board's parking lot she exclaims: I win! The other three demonstrate dismay at having lost.

Dismay at having lost, or just dismay at having spent an hour of their precious, irreplaceable youth playing Mall Madness?

Truck nuts

Reaction to these accessories has been mixed.

Some dismissed them as a classless and trashy accessory that likely violated public decency laws. For others, the first time they saw truck nuts, the heavens opened up as a celestial choir of cherubim and seraphim descended a-trumpeting, bearing molded plastic in the shape of testicles, all the better to complement the majestic glory of their "Calvin peeing on the Yankees logo" decal.

So, yeah, mixed.

The Good, the Bad, and Huckleberry Hound

Kevin Costner was inspired to write Dances With Wolves after viewing this movie on television.

Is this obviously just a piece of vandalism? Yes. Does the image it conjures up—of an unshaven, underwear-clad Costner watching Hanna-Barbera cartoons with a bowl of Crunch Berries in his lap while he tries to stave off writer's block and futilely attempts to get his agent to return his calls—make it totally worth including in this book? Absolutely.

http://en.wikipedia.org/wiki/The_Good,_the_Bad,_and_Huckleberry_Hound

Narwhal

Narwhals that have been brought into captivity tend to die.

Sadly, narwhals that spend their entire lives in the ocean also tend to die.

http://en.wikipedia.org/wiki/Narwhal

The Craft (film)

According to BoxOfficeMojo.com, The Craft is the 7th highest grossing movie since 1980 dealing with the genre of witches.

> *Or, as a human being might say* "The Craft *is a movie about some witches.*"

Steve Buckhantz

Buckhantz's catchphrases have seeped into the lexicon of Washington, D.C. area sports fans, who revel in using them to describe a myriad of non-sports related events (ex. males observing a friend attempting to ask a woman for her phone number exclaim[citation needed] "Dagger!" or "Backbreaker!" when she can be seen rejecting the friend's advances) as well as debating the subtle and compelling distinction between a "Backbreaker" (a made basket at a critical juncture in a game that breaks any chance that the opposing team will win) and a "Dagger" (a made basket at a critical juncture in a game that stabs like a dagger at the opposing team's chance of victory).

The types of people who have the time to debate the "subtle and compelling" differences between a sports announcer's catchphrases often find themselves getting to apply those same catchphrases towards a wide variety of real-life social rejections.

http://en.wikipedia.org/wiki/Steve_Buckhantz

Tortellini

The origin of tortellini is surrounded by several legends.[citation needed]

> *The most famous of them is "The Legend of the Interesting Origin of the Incredibly Mundane Item," but most historians conclude that this legend has no factual basis.*

Mesoamerican ballgame

Even without human sacrifice, the game could be brutal.

> *Just imagine some poor, disappointed kid kicking the dirt as they leave their first, sacrifice-free Mesoamerican ballgame: "Yeah ... it was **kinda** brutal ... I guess...."*

http://en.wikipedia.org/wiki/Mesoamerican_ballgame

No Money

Realizing that he has started off on the wrong foot by raping Ayase after the auction, he tries to make it up to him by doing various things with mixed results.

*Playing Monopoly with him? Successful. Baking him oatmeal cookies? Not so much. (Turns out Ayase doesn't care for oatmeal.) What still nags at him, though, is the possibility that everything would have turned out fine if he'd raped Ayase after the **garage sale**, rather than after the auction.*

Autograph hobby timeline

2001: The September 11 terrorist attacks raise airport security levels, making it difficult for the public to approach celebrities for autographs at U.S. airports.

Nobody suffered more on that horrible day than the people who had been planning to get an autograph from the guy who plays Jay from Jay and Silent Bob *when he got off an airplane on September 12th.*

Lippy the Lion & Hardy Har Har

The latter's name is ironic, as it's an onomatopoeia for laughter, and Hardy is an eternal pessimist, Hardy is the stereotype of someone with a very deep Major depressive disorder; indeed, one short implies that expression of joy or happiness actually puts Hardy in pain.

The expression of joy or happiness has the same effect on Rupert Murdoch.

Pac-Man

In December 1982, an 8-year-old boy, Jeffrey R. Yee, supposedly received a letter from U.S. President Ronald Reagan congratulating him on a worldwide record of 6,131,940 points, a score only possible if he had passed the Split-Screen Level. Whether or not this event happened as described has remained in heated debate among video-game circles since its supposed occurrence.

> When forced to testify before the Senate Committee on Video Game Excellence on this important issue, Reagan gave responses that were variations of "I can't recall" seventeen times over the course of half an hour of questioning.

http://en.wikipedia.org/wiki/Pac-Man

The Brady Bunch in the White House

The film begins with Bobby finding a winning lottery ticket, that Mike insists must be returned to its rightful owner. The White House Press Secretary finds out about this and, to boost sagging approval ratings, invites the Bradys to the White House as reward for their honesty. Soon afterward, the President of the United States abandons his post, thus leaving his staff to come up with a wholesome, all-American replacement: the Bradys. Mike Brady is appointed as President; Carol Brady, in addition to being the First Lady, becomes the first female Vice President; and the new "First Family" moves into the White House. Along the way, a giant asteroid is heading for Earth. Greg has a fling with Veronica, and writes her a song (small excerpt) "Veronica, Veronica, Veronica, Veronica, Veronica, Veronica, Veronica, Veronica."

The Brady administration's more hawkish policies were spearheaded by Alice, who can be heard on secretly recorded White House tapes ordering the Air Force to "turn Laos into a parking lot."

http://en.wikipedia.org/wiki/The_Brady_Bunch_in_the_White_House

Gee-haw whammy diddle

Sometimes also known as a "Ouija Windmill", a "Hooey Stick" or a "VooDoo Stick". The word "Whammy" is sometimes "Whimmy" and the word "Diddle" sometimes "Doodle", giving it a possible 3 other names, and the "Gee-Haw" may also be dropped.

No matter what you call it, it's still the best-selling home pregnancy test on the market.

http://en.wikipedia.org/wiki/Gee-haw_whammy_diddle

Do you know where your children are?

In a Garfield strip from September 1, 1986, Jon hears this said on the 10 o'clock news after Garfield and Odie have run away. He bursts into tears.

Many critics acknowledge this as the funniest thing that has ever happened in a Garfield *comic strip.*

The Rain in Spain

Spanish rain does not actually stay mainly in the plain. It falls mainly in the northern mountains.

File this little "fun fact" under "things to tell women if the next thing you want to hear out of their mouth is 'I have a boyfriend.'"

Islamic toilet etiquette

While on the toilet, one must remain silent. Talking, answering greetings or greeting others is strongly discouraged. When defecating together, two men cannot converse, nor look at each other's private parts, and especially not handle each other's private parts.

Zoroastrians, on the other hand, are a bunch of chatty genital-touchers.

http://en.wikipedia.org/wiki/Islamic_toilet_etiquette

Cletus Spuckler

In The Simpsons Hit & Run Cletus appears in several missions including finding road kill or harvesting ketchup but at end of 'Ketchup Logic' there is a clip were Cletus says 'my grandpapa done see one of those seed drawing (crop circles) once, but he's with Allah now. This could hint Cletus is Muslim but this is unlikely.

Mostly because of Cletus's tendency to handle other men's private parts while defecating.

Robert the Doll

The dolls hair also changed colour which is impossible because after hair is cut it can't change colour.

And yet Robert the Doll somehow managed to do so, making the toy an unholy abomination that violated the natural order of the universe, and also came with its own pacifier.

http://en.wikipedia.org/wiki/Robert_the_Doll

Dastardly and Muttley in Their Flying Machines

Muttley (voiced by Don Messick) is Dastardly's bungling canine sidekick. He rarely speaks, and when he does it usually takes the form of either (1) just cursing to himself indistinctly, usually following some misfortune that has befallen him, or (2) an excited "yeah-yeah-yeah..." at the offer of something appealing or in response to a command/request from Dastardly. There are times when distinct single words can be discerned amid his mutterings (e.g., "Sassafrassarassa Chicken Zilly").

Important note: If the person sitting next to you on a Greyhound bus ever curses to themself indistinctly, excitedly says "yeah-yeah-yeah," or mutters "Sassafrassarassa Chicken Zilly" under their breath, do not compliment them on their "great Muttley impression." They will cut you.

Timeline of the burrito

1840

Burrito created in 1840s American Southwest/ Northwestern Mexico. Spiced meat wrapped in flour tortillas made popular by gold miners who worked with burros. Janey M. Rifkin in Hispanic Times Magazine claims this was the original source of meat. If true, it would be out of desperation; burro meat is not considered palatable[citation needed]

When modern inhabitants of the American Southwest turn to a particular kind of burrito filling out of desperation, it's usually at Taco Bell.

http://en.wikipedia.org/wiki/Timeline_of_the_burrito

List of As Told by Ginger characters

Mrs. Killgallen

It has never been clear if a Mrs. Killgallen, 42 years old, even exists as she has never been mentioned.

> *The Wikipedia equivalent of "What is the sound of one hand clapping?"*

Fire in the hole

The phrase has also been used to describe the act of throwing hot food or drink in the face of a store or restaurant worker as a prank.

Another popular "prank" involves shooting out the tires of the ambulance transporting the burned worker to the hospital, then driving to their home and strangling their pet dog.

http://en.wikipedia.org/wiki/Fire_in_the_hole

Zev (horse)

Bred by the famous horseman John E. Madden, Zev was owned by the Rancocas Stable of Harry F. Sinclair, the founder of Sinclair Oil, who was a central figure in the Teapot Dome scandal under Warren G. Harding, President of the United States. Harding died mysteriously in San Francisco before the scandal hit, but Sinclair went through the worst of it, serving time in prison for selling US oil reserves to private interests for his own personal aggrandizement.

But before all that, Sinclair named the horse Zev in honor of his friend and personal lawyer, Colonel Zevely.

Terribly written, but be let's honest: it's the most interesting thing you've ever read about the Teapot Dome Scandal.

http://en.wikipedia.org/wiki/Zev_(horse)

Friday

Friday is the day between Thursday and Saturday.

> *But what the hell are Thursday and Saturday?!*

http://en.wikipedia.org/wiki/Friday

Bikini car wash

Depending on the organization responsible, as well as the local laws, a variation of the bikini car wash sometimes occurs, in which the women will wash the car topless, usually for an extra fee. This type of car wash is not found in the US as part of any legitimate charitable or fund raising event[citation needed].

Wikipedia? The UNICEF Double D's for Darfur topless car wash would like a word with you.

http://en.wikipedia.org/wiki/Car_wash#Bikini_car_wash

Princess Ozma

Another story in which Ozma acquires a boyfriend is the "Dan in Oz" series by David Hardenbrook, which stars a young and lovable computer geek named Dan Maryk. Other such romances exist among unpublished fan fiction.

> ***More*** *unpublished fan fiction exists featuring computer geeks getting women? No [citation needed] tag necessary. Never in our lives have we been so certain that something is true.*

Home run

When two consecutive batters each hit a home run, this is described as back-to-back home runs. It is still considered back-to-back even if both batters hit their home runs off different pitchers. A third batter hitting a home run is commonly referred to as back-to-back-to-back. Four home runs in a row by consecutive batters has only occurred seven times in the history of Major League Baseball. Following convention, this is called back-to-back-to-back-to-back.

Advanced theorists have speculated as to what it would be called were a fifth batter to hit a consecutive home run. One possible term that has been put forth is "chicken bake," but these arguments rarely reach a consensus, and often involve bloodshed.

Valmont (film)

Valmont opened to mixed reception in its day. While Dangerous Liaisons was liked for its hard working stars, Valmont was considered not half as good. The stars, according to critics, were good, but the story was not quite realized and seemed a little unreal. Others felt the movie did not hit the mark as it should have.

Dangerous Liasons *won Oscars for Best Adapted Screenplay, Costume Design, and Art Direction, but was egregiously snubbed in the category of Hardest Working Stars.*

Valmont, *on the other hand, received further criticism for its deceptive selective editing of the pull quote "'The stars were good' –Critics" on its movie poster, though it sensibly omitted quotes such as "'The movie did not hit the mark as it should have' –Others."*

http://en.wikipedia.org/wiki/Valmont_(film)

Beast (comics)

Beast later uncovers what seems to be a female mutant with feline features, like his situation. This raises hopes for him, until he discovers it's not a mutant female that looks like a cat, it's a mutant cat who looks like a human.

Though Beast tells himself that looks are only skin deep, he knows deep down that how you appear to the outside world is more important than anybody wants to let on. Meeting a female mutant that looks like a cat could be the only opportunity he has to bond with someone on a higher level and, by transcending the limits of physical attraction, finally achieve true happiness.

*Wait, it's actually a mutant **cat** who looks like a **human**? Oh, God, what does he look like, a perv?!*

http://en.wikipedia.org/wiki/Beast_(comics)

Happy Birthday to You

It is often the tradition that at a birthday party, the song "Happy Birthday to You" is sung with the birthday person seated in front of a table where there is a birthday cake with candles that have just been lit, with the other guests gathered around. The number of candles is often the same as the age of the birthday person. After the song is sung (usually just once), sometimes party guests will add phrase like "And many happy returns!" or "And many more!" expressing the hope that the birthday person will enjoy a long life. The birthday person is asked to make a wish ("Make a wish!") — which is done silently — and then blow out the candles. Traditionally, the blowing out of the candles is felt to signify that the wish will come true. Once the candles have been blown out, people often will applaud, and then the cake is usually served — often by the birthday person — and eaten.

Often, after the cake is eaten, each guest gives a gift, usually wrapped in festive paper, to the birthday person. Often the birthday person will then open the gifts, revealing their contents to all. That usually concludes the ritual aspect of a birthday party, which then proceeds much like any other but with the birthday person being treated as the guest of honor.[citation needed]

> *Imagine how terrifying it would be if you discovered your dog were taking notes like this to report back to his home planet.*

http://en.wikipedia.org/wiki/Happy_Birthday_to_You

Master of Social Work

The Master of Social Work (MSW) is a master's degree in social work.

Please consider another field of study if this is news to you.

http://en.wikipedia.org/wiki/Master_of_Social_Work

E.T. the Extra-Terrestrial (video game)

The game ends when the energy bar depletes, or the player decides to quit.

You want to know what's terrifying? That quote from the Wikipedia article about the E.T. Atari game just as accurately sums up the entirety of a human life. If you need us, we'll be sitting on the corner of our bed, staring at the wall in silence.

http://en.wikipedia.org/wiki/E.T._the_Extra-Terrestrial_(video_game)

About the Authors

Josh Fruhlinger is the creator of the Comics Curmudgeon, a surprisingly successful blog that makes fun of *Mary Worth* and *Apartment 3-G* and proves that pretty much anyone can become mildly famous on the Internet for any reason whatsoever, as long as they update every day. He's also written for the satirical political blog Wonkette, recorded a RiffTrax, and finished in third place on his only *Jeopardy!* appearance (the correct answer was "Golda Meir"). He lives in Baltimore with his wife Amber and his cat Hoagie.

Conor Lastowka has written for RiffTrax.com for the majority of its existence. He founded the fake holiday National High Five Day, plays bass in his fake band Re-Ree, and hosts the all too real [Citation Needed] Podcast. He lives in San Diego with his wife Lauren and his cat Slidell.

Like what you've just read?
Get more [Citation Needed]!

Blog: citationneeded.tumblr.com
Podcast: citationneeded.tumblr.com/thepodcast
(or search "citation needed" on iTunes)
Twitter: twitter.com/cit8tionneeded
Facebook: facebook.com/citationneeded

Made in the USA
Charleston, SC
17 November 2011